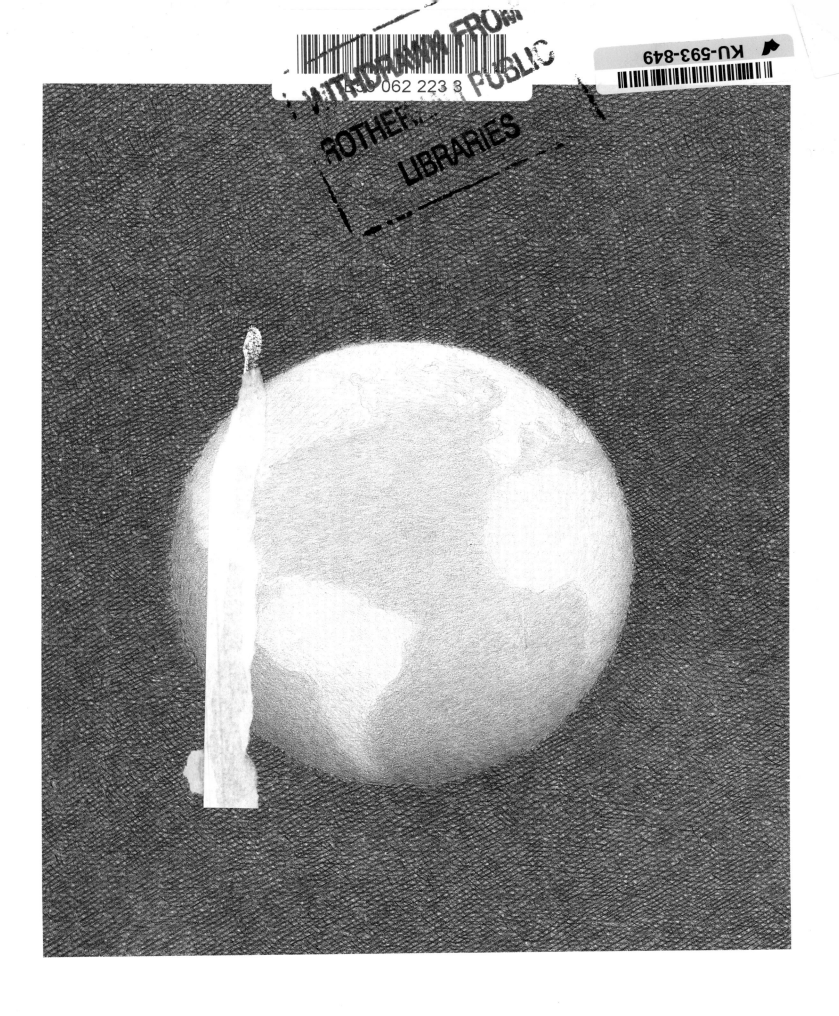

For TC, with love
 N. D.

For Olivia Isabel Conley and Toby Foster Stubbings
 P. B.

Nick Dowson is an author and teacher who is passionate about natural history. He has written two books for Walker's Nature Storybook series, *Tracks of a Panda* and *Tigress*. About writing *North*, he says, "One windswept Christmas in the Shetland Isles, I had a taste of Arctic winter. Here's where my journey north began…" Nick lives with his wife in Suffolk.

Patrick Benson has illustrated many children's books, including *The Sea-Thing Child* by Russell Hoban and *Owl Babies* by Martin Waddell, which has sold over three million copies. He has won both the Mother Goose Award and the Kurt Maschler Award for his work. Patrick lives in the Scottish Borders with his family, and says, "Watching the skeins of geese fly north in the spring, I wish I could go with them to experience a summer in the Arctic … but I'd be sure to pack my mosquito repellent!"

WALKER BOOKS
AND SUBSIDIARIES
LONDON · BOSTON · SYDNEY · AUCKLAND

First published 2011 by Walker Books Ltd, 87 Vauxhall Walk, London SE11 5HJ • This edition published 2013 • 10 9 8 7 6 5 4 3 2 1 • Text © 2011 Nick Dowson • Illustrations © 2011 Patrick Benson • The right of Nick Dowson and Patrick Benson to be identified as author and illustrator respectively of this work has been asserted by them in accordance with the Copyright, Designs and Patents Act 1988 • This book has been typeset in Gill Sans • Printed in China • All rights reserved. No part of this book may be reproduced, transmitted or stored in an information retrieval system in any form or by any means, graphic, electronic or mechanical, including photocopying, taping and recording, without prior written permission from the publisher. • British Library Cataloguing in Publication Data: a catalogue record for this book is available from the British Library. • ISBN 978-1-4063-4403-5 • www.walker.co.uk

# NORTH

## The Greatest Animal Journey on Earth

by Nick Dowson • illustrated by Patrick Benson

AT THE VERY TOP
OF OUR WORLD

is a huge wild place

called the Arctic.

Here in winter, the sun

sinks away,

blizzards fill the darkness

and even the seas

freeze deep.

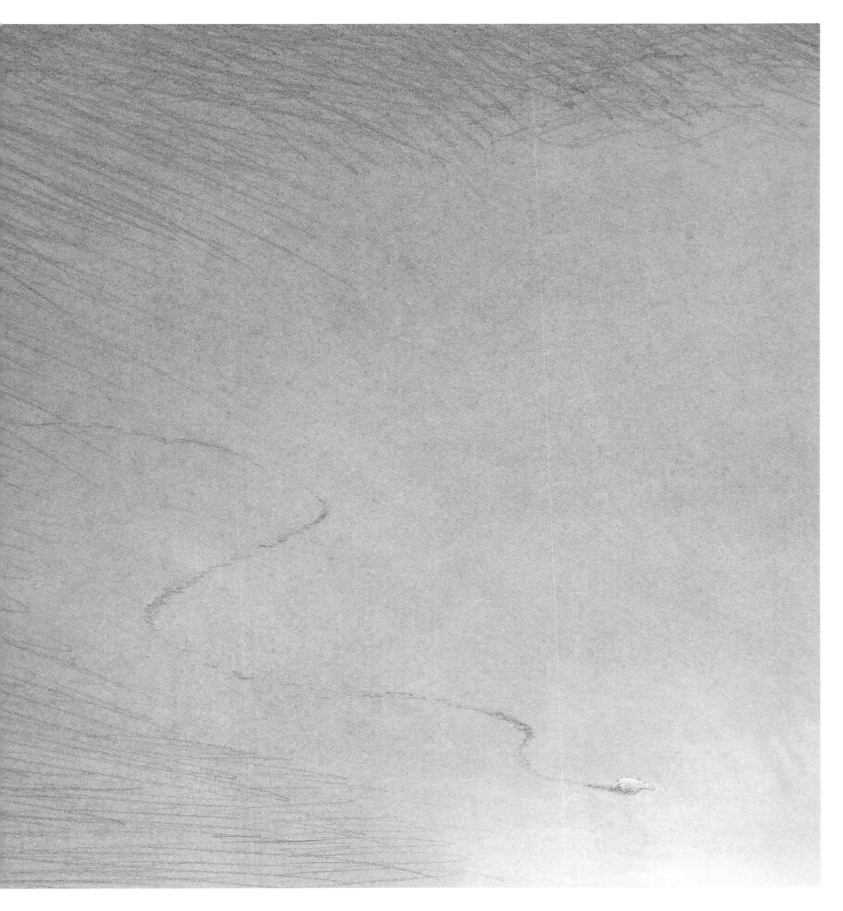

Then the Arctic is like
an icy desert.
Only animals like polar bear
and arctic fox –
with coats of fur to keep
the cold away –
can stay alive.

But when spring comes,
bringing back the sun
with light and warmth,
the Arctic changes.

Beneath its frozen seas,
tiny algae begin to bloom
on the undersides of ice,
colouring it golden brown.

While on land, plants creep up
through melting snow,
turning the tundra green.

For now, fox and bear
search for food alone.
But not for long ...
soon visitors will come.

Each year, in spring, many
kinds of animal travel
to the Arctic.
They come because they know
there will be lots to eat
and space to feed and breed
and roam in.

From right across the world,
millions risk everything
to fly, walk or swim here.

IT IS THE GREATEST
JOURNEY ON EARTH!

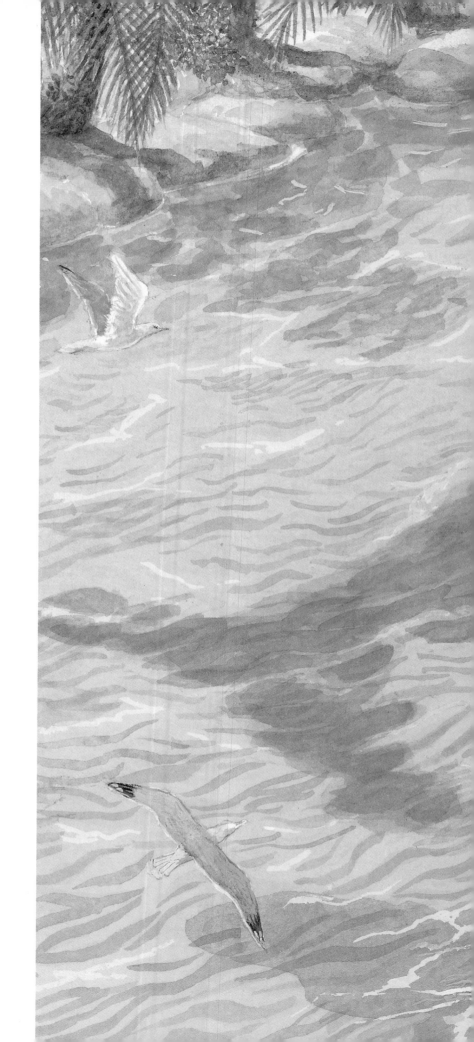

SOME OF THE FIRST TO LEAVE
ON THEIR JOURNEY
are grey whales.
This one is young.

Water slides over her
barnacled head
as she glides through the blue
of a Mexican lagoon –
over crabs and sand,
past boats, other whales
and out into the cold roll
of the Pacific Ocean.

For eight long weeks,
she'll swim north
without feeding ...

past Los Angeles,

San Francisco,

Vancouver Island,

Anchorage – and into the Arctic Circle.

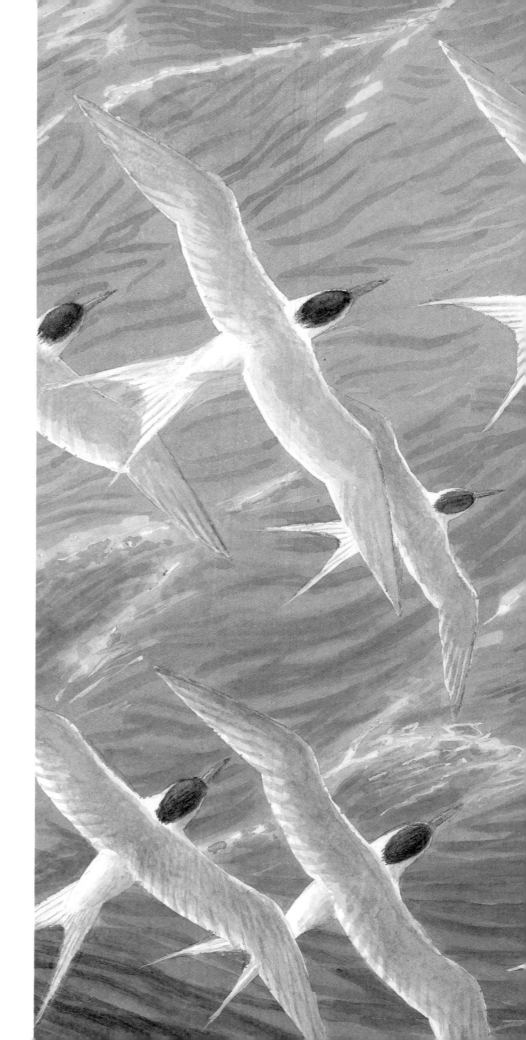

Five thousand miles
the grey whales swim,
but these birds travel
        twice as far.

From Antarctica, in March,
at the southern tip of
        the world,
terns are on their way.

Unlike the grey whales,
they feed as they go.
Their sharp eyes see sudden
twists of silver and they dive.

Above them,
        bigger birds wait.
These skuas bully terns
        to steal their fish:
bully them all the way
        to the Arctic…

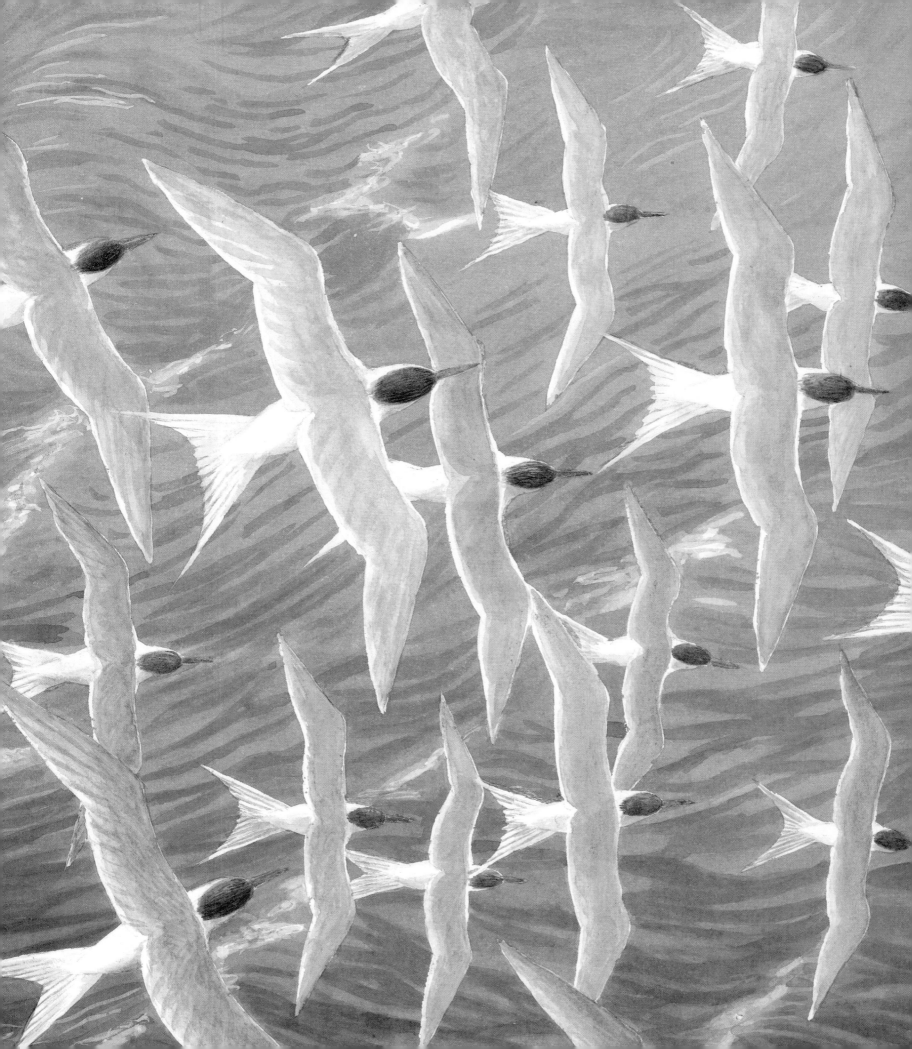

Other birds, too, are getting ready to head north.
Before take-off, they fuel up to fly.

On a sheltered New Zealand shore, a pair of bar-tailed godwits
sink their bills into the silt – for insects, shrimp and shellfish.

Snow geese grub a stubble field in Mexico

for grains of wasted corn.

At the edge of a Chinese lake, white cranes graze.

Their long legs step like ballerinas'. Their huge bills tear up roots to eat.

Some fly, some swim,
while others walk
    the journey north.

These pregnant caribou
have left the dark
    Canadian forests
where they wintered.

As they trek through
    deep snow
and cross cold
    swollen rivers,
their coats of hollow hair
keep them warm
and help them to swim.

28

Grey wolves slink after them,
    watching for weakness,
hoping a lame one might
    make a meal.

When the herd nears the sea,
four hundred miles
    further north,
there will be fresh leaves
    and shoots to eat.

Safe on higher ground,
    the caribou will calve.

Not far away,
a month-old Pacific walrus calf
slides after his big, blubbery mother
into the cold April sea.

She'll lead him slowly
up the coast of Alaska,
hungry for shellfish
from the Arctic Ocean's floor.

Smaller swimmers, too,
fill the northern seas.
After spawning, this silver
   herring shoal heads north,
to feed on clouds
of blooming plankton.

With bright scales like mirrors,
they swerve together,
fin to fin.

Behind them drift their fry:
trillions of tiny fish
   carried by the current
in the May Norwegian Sea.

And grey-tusked
   narwhal whales,
strange as fairytales,
join the journey
north to Spitzbergen...

BY LATE MAY, TRAVELLERS
CROWD TOGETHER
near the very top of the world,
where even
the coldest frozen seas
are melting.

Ice sheets crack and split,
and bowhead whales
break up the slabs with
their thick, bony skulls.

New sea lanes teem
with creatures
streaming north –

as far as they can go –

to reach their journey's end…

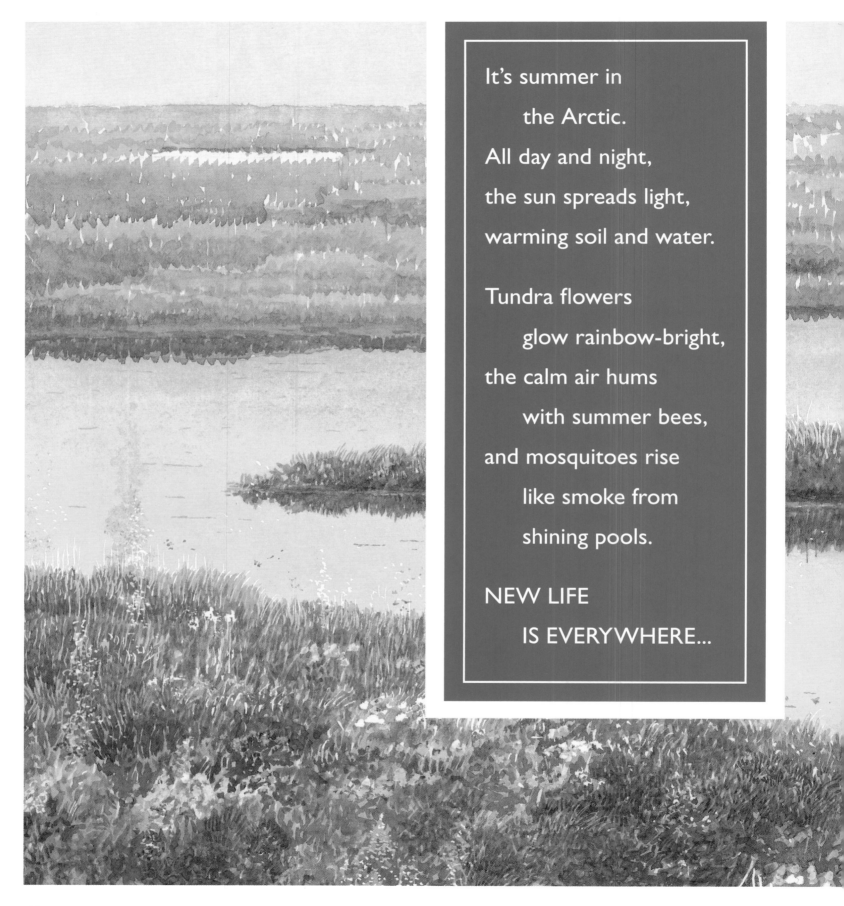

It's summer in
     the Arctic.
All day and night,
the sun spreads light,
warming soil and water.

Tundra flowers
     glow rainbow-bright,
the calm air hums
     with summer bees,
and mosquitoes rise
     like smoke from
     shining pools.

NEW LIFE
     IS EVERYWHERE...

But then September comes.

The days grow shorter.

Sunlight dims and winds begin to blow.

While young terns and goslings,
  cranes and godwits

test their wings, whales and walrus
  are filling up with food.

Soon all the visitors will journey south –

back to where they winter...

Ice stills the sea.
Snow fills the land.
Winter grips the Arctic
     once again.

Now polar bear
     and fox, musk ox
and arctic hare roam
     the frozen night alone.

But not for long…

Always the sun comes
warming back in spring.
And, once more,
around the world,
the wild migration
will begin –

FOR THE GREATEST
JOURNEY ON EARTH!

## About the Arctic

The Arctic is not a continent, but an ocean region that includes thousands of islands and the northern parts of North America, Europe and Asia.

It is an area of about 14,056,000 square kilometres – roughly the size of Russia.

The Arctic is the second coldest place on Earth. In winter, the sun never rises and temperatures sink to -40°C.

In much of the Arctic, it is too cold and windy for trees to grow, but low-lying flowering plants can survive.

Not many animals can live all year round in the Arctic. Those that do include polar bears, arctic foxes, musk oxen and arctic hares. Each year, in spring, over 180 kinds of animal migrate from other parts of the world and join them.

The ocean closest to the North Pole (where it is coldest) stays permanently frozen. It's called the icecap.

Recently, global warming has caused the icecap to start melting, threatening some native Arctic animals with extinction, especially polar bears.

Warmer Arctic sea water also threatens plankton – the main source of food for the birds, whales and fish that migrate there.

Find out more about the Arctic online:
**www.mnh.si.edu**
**www.discoveringthearctic.org.uk**

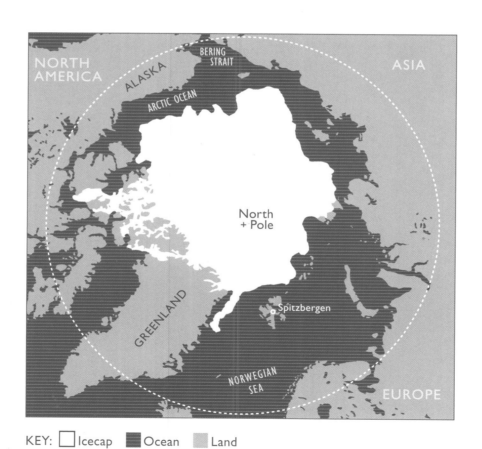

KEY: ☐ Icecap ■ Ocean ■ Land

## Glossary

**Algae** – simple plants without roots that grow in sunlit water

**Arctic Circle** – an imaginary line on maps that goes around the Arctic region

**Blizzard** – a violent snowstorm with cold, strong winds

**Extinction** – when a particular plant or animal dies out for ever

**Fry** – baby fish hatched from eggs

**Global warming** – when the average temperature of the earth rises

**Ice sheet** – a giant layer of frozen water

**Migration** – when large numbers of animals travel long distances to feed or breed

**Plankton** – tiny plants and animals that drift near the surface of the sea

**Sea lane** – a path across the sea through melting ice

**Silt** – fine grains of mud, sand and stone that lie at the bottom of ocean or river beds

**Spawning** – when fish lay their eggs in water

**Tundra** – a treeless plain with soil that stays frozen, except in summer, when enough melts for plants to grow

## Index

Arctic fox 6, 11, 50
Arctic hare 50
Bar-tailed godwits 22–23, 46–47
Caribou 26–29, 44–45
Grey wolves 28–29
Herring 32–33
Musk ox 50–51
Polar bears 6–7, 11, 50
Plankton 33
Shoots 29
Skuas 18, 20–21
Snow geese 24–25
Spring 8, 11, 52
Summer 40–45
Sun 4, 8, 40, 52
Terns 18–21, 46
Walrus 30–31, 42–43, 46–47
White cranes 24–25, 46
Whales, bowhead, 36–37;
    grey, 12–17, 18;
    narwhal, 33, 34–35
Winter 4, 46, 50